WORLD AS YOU LEFT IT

WORLD AS YOU LEFT IT

POEMS

Helen Wickes

SIXTEEN
RIVERS PRESS

My thanks to Sixteen Rivers Press; the Whitmaniacs writing group and
David St. John; Richard Silberg and Joyce Jenkins of *Poetry Flash*;
Lloyd Schwartz, Marguerite Cunningham, Cynthia Keiser, Babette Jenny,
Eve Pell, Carolyn Miller, Lynne Knight, Murray Silverstein, and Gillian Wegener;
my brothers Michael and Timothy Wickes; and Don Stang.

Thanks to Tree Swenson for permission to use the quote from Liam Rector's
poem, "Toast," from his book *American Prodigal.*

Published by Sixteen Rivers Press
P.O. Box 640663
San Francisco, CA 94164-0663
www.sixteenrivers.org

Library of Congress Control Number: 2014950632
ISBN 978-1-939639-08-0

Design: Josef Beery
Cover photographs: Michael Wickes

For Don

To memory, that enormous bowl of water.
To what we imagined, what sent us off.
To that pitcher which poured us.

—Liam Rector, from "Toast"

Contents

SO I STOLE IT

Walking after Sunrise

I'd go out walking your dogs, the both of them, big bruisers,
and everyone knows I don't like dogs —
the smell, the noise, and the drool of them — that year
and a half you two spent dying, and I traveled
the miles for the chance to see you, to be with you,
to harvest every small thing for memory's larder.
I walked your loony beasts, their electric collars
keeping them on a virtual leash; mornings, off we'd go

into the cold air's bright teeth, to the snowy field,
the whole world enormous and quiet just this side
of what was approaching, while your pets, they peed
and galloped, sniffed and pooped, the sky was blue,
the winter landscape folding all of us into memory —
you, me, thin sunlight, and the goofy, delirious dogs.

New Moon over Jennersville

The cold snow blowing sideways,
whole sky opening wide over the fields;
he's dying a few miles back there.
Just for tonight I leave the dying
and the living who tend to them
and stop my car to watch the Amish guy
with his team of flaxen-maned chestnuts
churn the cornstalks through new falling snow—
and three crows desultory across the sky,
snow now quitting, the sunset brilliant
this final day in January. But, oh Lord,
please spare me another Norah Jones song
on the radio tonight, to hell with her ship,
her flag, her wailing. Wherever home is,
tonight, I'm on my way.

The Year with a Hole in the Center

He walks with a cane so as to chase the gravel,
which trips him up. *Who am I,*
he asks. *Who are you, do I know you?*
Tip-tap of the cane; I could live on chocolate and air.

The summer sun through the damp air is a greasy stain,
the whole sky sliding through its chosen universe.

If there's any heaven at all, I've got my ticket,
if there's no heaven, I've still got my ticket,
I'm going there too.

        ~

My father takes back his adoration for the world, refusing
to name the dog Max, the horse Hawk, the smell
of bacon, the nearly weightless ice clinking in the tea.

Even the six stars — count them — six stars at night,
   and downstairs, the fireflies,
aren't they just a whole cityscape, as seen from above,
on a long flight home from far away?
I remember almost nothing of childhood, and neither does he.

        ~

But oh, was he precise about how to clean a horse's tail:
never with a brush, *Use your goddamn fingers, one strand*
one hair at a time, until you're combing
through silk.

To be world-weary is to want to die, but never before sunset.
To grieve alone is to fester, but to grieve in public
is to enter the tide.

A waste of life and talent is really no matter.

At the end when his mind slithered out of time, he wound
the fat rubber bands, twenty, thirty-five,
around his hospital cane. Around five hospital canes.
To protect them.

∼

In the hospital he was tied like a madman, hands and feet to the bed.

I was summoned from my hotel and he called out,
Did you bring the knife to cut me out of here?
Well, no—and he said, *You stupid, goddamn*
silly nitwit of an idiot, to which gesture

there was only one answer—to grab his shoulders and looking
into his green eyes, say, *You stupid son of a bitch, don't ever*
fucking talk to me like that. Like that.

It might have been exhilarating, but no, of course, it was
a sad and very small thing to do and to be.

~

In two months he could walk the fence line, the cane in one hand,
the broom in the other.

Four old bay geldings gallop to the fence, wheel and halt.
Hawk whinnies, Chinook rolls on one side, jumps up
and rolls on the other. *You own them,* I say. — *Oh yeah?*

In spring, to keep his balance, he counts the buttercups underfoot,
in summer, to keep ahold of his mind, he counts the dandelions.
Only when a life is done
does it claim its shape from the myriad possible shapes
it has been choosing all along.

Twice a day, the gravel must be swept, and again, and although
there is no blessedness to grow toward, there surely is,
and this must be, purgatory. For those of us
who are summoned to watch and wait.

His fear recedes except when the leaves lift up, not a breeze
to be felt for miles, his eyes tighten against the onrush,
to the brink, to the *wham,* the *kaput,* the *empty.*
Though the four bay geldings call out to him, he cannot name them.

~

Late, he was always late, his pickup squealing
around the corner, and to really piss me off, the hay bales
stuck with pitchforks, two yowling mutts,
the cigarette throwing yips of flame,
but alas, I'm the only wrong one here — wrong coat, wrong hair,
wrong shoes, all wrong to that smug suburban-kid life — and him
shrugging, *To hell with the lousy lot of them.*

He drops my brother and me at the orchard, with a gunnysack,
to crawl under the barbed wire, to loot the ripest apples,
and watch out for the bees, the yellow jackets, the wasps,
the owner and *his friggin' dogs,*

not because, I much later realized, we couldn't afford the apples,
but for pure sport, and *to sharpen our poor, dumb-ass kid brains,*

and we had all the racket to boot, the cicadas and crickets
drowning the warm September air, the distant Phillies game
on his radio, the tinny engine we were forever running toward.

Spelling It Out

The geese are doing weird things
across the January sky. After collapsing their V
into chaos, it looks as if they want to form
another letter, which they move toward, and failing
to configure, they settle back into V.
I guess it's a mid-air place to come home to.

But to hell with the geese — there's ice on the pond,
and mist from the mouths of dogs
barking as the east turns pink,
and the last stars retreat, and how, in the end,
he keeps himself alive for her. For her

the labored breathing, the mind prone to babble,
the body's husk hanging on. For her the yellow pill,
then the blue one. Some of us whisper
as we spoon him the orange Jell-O, *You can
go now, we'll take care of her. For you.*

But he's not believing a word we say.
We uncover his swollen feet and rub them.
We describe the fumbling aerial scribble of the geese,
how it looks like they're trying to spell out something
true. *If there is another world, you can go there, now,*
we tell him, with hope and with

considerable self-loathing, and to forestall
how the world might still get back at us,
we correct ourselves, saying, *Don't go today, don't
leave us today.* The sun lights up the barn, the house,
the road, and lights up the broad backs
of four bay horses grazing, again.

November Chill and All the Animals

The goat man's moved his herd
across the valley, and it resembles a cloud
drifting across and chewing the buckskin hillside.

The oak trees squat low as if afraid of the sky.
Whatever breathed us here is breathing us back today,
which feels like being gathered,
whether we like it or not.

First curry, then brush. Then burrs from the mane,
and the tail untangled by hand.
This black hair is wrapped around my wrist —
past the dead deer slung by the fence,
and all the goats not seeming to mind.

With a tobacco wad in the left side of his mouth,
five nails in the other,
Joel the farrier is saying that his mule
won't cross creeks. Joel asks
if I like goat — *no. What's tougher,* he asks,
elk or antelope? I say that antelope needs marinade.

He pares the hoof back to a naked greeny white.
Such small feet. The warm breath of the horse
rummaging my clothes. One crow, then another,
calls out, and the three of us stop to listen.

Loot

So I stole it, oh yes I did, stole my father's address book.
And look — the girls —
       A *Doris*, two *Bettys*, and a *Hazel*,
From '36, in a little brown leather thing,
       Full of *Gladys* and *Louise*, *Edith* at *Tuxedo 2-080*,
From his dresser drawer — him in the next room sleeping and waking
And asking where he was. I'd gone rifling for a handkerchief

And found this piece of him, age twenty-one, acquainted with *Ina*,
       And *(Red-Haired) Sonya*, known to guys like
       Billy, Jack, and *Eddie (pal of Lamont)*.
He had written with his fountain pen — *1 honey, 1 lemon juice,*
       4 rum, and later — *Harlem: The Radium Club,*
       Next door to Cotton Club, underlined and bold

In faded ink. How could I *not* steal this, and wouldn't you
Have done the same, when the opening page read,
       This is damned Private — and this means you.
Means me? Starved for the gleanings of history,
Even the names and numbers of, oh Lord, another *Gladys*,

       A *Babs*, and that *(Beaut. Blond) Doris*. Where'd they end up,
Ladies known to a guy who sang, *Be a rootie-toot-tootie,*
Find yourself a cutie, what's the rest? He can't remember.
       Have I lost my mind? he asked again today.
Only some of it, I answered, *like me.*

~

Who was *Frances* or *Iris* at *Schuyler 5-138* to a guy
Who didn't seem to care that much for people, who liked
His good dog, his horse, or a fat bird he'd shot and gutted,
    Roasted, and eaten. Who preferred thinking
About the light, how it alters — flattens and yellows —
    Before a tornado strikes.

~

I can't make out this coded stuff — the squiggles beside
    Jack and *Fred* — his dope guys, I wonder,
Or maybe his bookies from Jersey — I knew about them.
But these bits I've scavenged from '36. His first wife,
A year down the road, my mother not even on the horizon,
This year when the doors of the world were flung wide

    For *Lilian* and *April, Callie* and *Lucille*, before
The men came home from Spain and fired him up
About *over there's* descent into hell, but all that
Was later. Now I remember the words — *Why should you*
    Be snootie, Just get your something — *sweet patootie.*

Mine to ponder, these hints and colors.
I'd like to sit down at the counter for lunch
    at *Adam's Chili House, 2 steps East of 7th.* And what
I wouldn't give to hear anything about *Loretta (Big Blond)*
Or *Thelma* at *Plaza 8-534.*

Before the Burial

Who says we can't read "The Shooting of Dan McGrew"
or some Damon Runyon. The preacher lady can handle it,
that's her calling, *or maybe we're her calling.*

Chambers, the backhoe guy, he's waiting for us out there now.

Right at the hedgerow, that's for his head, and to the east,
where his feet must go. So she can see from her bedroom window.

We'll have a lot of sandwiches, finger food.
Sad people get hungry too, *and get that cat off the table.*

Does this little black skirt make my butt look big? No, but
that ugly parka likens you to a whale. *Very like a whale.*

He asked to be put into the old pear orchard, a field
that hasn't seen a tree for forty years — which is
exactly what I told you — out in the old pear orchard.

If that lady preacher says *amazing landscape* a third time,
may I slap her, may I have some finger food?

A few of us have manners left, so please lock up the dogs
and lock up that cat. *I have always yearned for a calling.*

Chambers, the backhoe guy, said he saw deer poop out there,
and said he saved the sod, come spring, we'll see it green again.

No one told me there'd be a great big old flag. No one told us
we'd have to walk. No one told us we'd get a snowstorm.
Well, settle down and try some of this finger food.

He can't wear Birkenstocks and jammies in the snow. And she
let that child walk open-toed and high-heeled out there.

The sun rose, pink and fiery, the kind of sun he'd haul us
outside for, whining and shuffling in our pajamas. I remember that.
I don't—you people have either memory or imagination.

The dirt road curving uphill, three crows, and a rabbit.
The old snow crunching, as the new snow stings in quick flurries.

All of us breathing as we walk—small puffs in the morning air.

Roadside

Let's go find some fresh-picked, where you
can choose and weigh and pay, and oh Lord,
the place is still right there, so park it on up.
Imagine, there are people in this life who trust

that we'll drop our cash in the box. Go on and
yank the greenery, sniff the kernels, stroke the silk,
take a nibble. Was it milky as well as crunchy,
did you check for bugs? He'll eat five, maybe six,
me just the one, the rest—two each, and you—a half—
deeply odd, your barely eating a half—no matter,
leave the money, nothing sets a tired brain on fire
like end-of-summer corn. I'm tired. Drive me home.

November Sun

This morning the wild turkeys, a dozen of them
rushing in front of me, the blue-black glint
of their feathers afire in the early light. I love
the startle and strangeness of them, the archaic,

here-we-come-from-your-forebears scene, as they
barrel across the ice-slicked road, heads down,
uttering their small, weird noises, the guy birds
with pink wattles jiggling, the girls satiny dark.

Here I go again, alive, squealing my brakes,
rolling down the window to see all I can see,
squinting into the cold morning sun's thin light,
so fierce in its strictures, so vast with its bounty.

KEEP THE STRINGS A-FLYING

Daedalus

I go on, and what else is a maker to do. I mourn, I go on.
My handiwork melted and disfigured before my eyes, beyond all
beauty and function as observed in the hummingbird, the vulture,

but he was my spawn, my foal, my own sweet fool
whom I launched, and he failed us both, he did.

For everything I make, something's unmade.

Hurled west—*old artificer*—I unfurled my fingertips, which ached
for the next thing of wonder fated for me to set loose,

as with my hands I made these—air lifters, sky sifters—pummeled
and pinched the wax, articulated each sinew, doomed as I am

to survive through my own sheer brilliance. Not my fault
he was dumb as a bag of hammers, but mine he was, and *it was*

my day. I'm uncontainable as air,
while he was of the more perishable earth. Of wren,

sparrow, hawk—the many nasty dead things I learned from—the owl
as well as the starling. I taught him to soar, to use the wind shift,
to float, dip, slice through clouds, but he screwed it up

and it wasn't my fault, now, was it? There were fields of gold
and I meant to see them all.

A father I was, but a maker too. And since these are the world's
perfect wings, I won't take flight with others, not ever.

And so we ascended, and he wasn't all that dumb, just heedless,
and I buried him, I mourned, I went on.

I fixed row upon row of feathers, precisely, as I saw
the journey, in my mind's eye, already existing, and it telling me
to follow. Fierce thing, the mind.

Day after Easter

Leaden sky, as it's called, bearing down,
mausoleum gray. Whatever was meant to be,
was, and if meant to rise, did that, too,
without or despite us. In the shops they're selling
turquoise eggs. I remember my mother
year after year at dawn, stooping to hide

her hand-dyed eggs, blue and green,
in plain sight. On her face such pleasure.
I think of Jay DeFeo painting
her radiant starburst rose for years,
thousands of pounds of paint, the paint
in some places nine inches thick,

poised as she was for years between the seen,
dripping from her paintbrush,
and the unseen she painted toward,
in brilliant white-gray bursting off the canvas,
out of the window, crossing the bay,
and merging with original light.

Atlas, running to fetch one apple,
the whole firmament briefly lifted from his back,
learned the meaning of weight
from one taste of lightness,
which is fragrant, a walled garden

whose trees blossom and fruit.
What this has to do with Easter
is that a dark, thick, cold day draws a line
at your feet. Dares you to back off,
dares you to smudge it.

Summer Heat

Sweet cherries of June come to market,
all purple-black and bursting open,
stem to seed, as if sunlight had bitten through them.
And oooh, these lady shoppers, so choosy,
pinching and fingering with delicate aggression,
until they've nabbed the perfect fruits.
Smoke and lazy laughter rise and swirl
from the barbecue down the street,

that whiff of normal life, trolling for takers.
From the dogwood, the frantic squirrel barks,
his hidden harvest eaten,
his new one unripe. The scent of musk-rose,
the garbage pail, and one swallow
swallowing the late light,
this light that's memory's handmaiden

hemming the end of the day
in fluid stitches. Memory of slippered feet
down the stairs, one tread whining, another one
whimpering, car door quietly closed, a small book
opened. I remember how the mind floats,
evading capture, a blown seedpod.
Outside, over and over, the shirring sound

of a skateboard clearing speed bumps —
two seconds of silence — the kid takes flight
and crashes down hard.

Marriage in the Atomic Age

He's broken the handle of the double boiler.

She's owned it forty years, permitting it to carry her
        from young to middle to old while it sat there

boiling, warming, steaming, as she sighed, whined,
sang, or muttered above the fumes; it was purchased

during the tenure of the ex or previous ex, who knows,
but this he, the best and final he, claims he'll fix it;

she says I'll find a craftsman, find some guy in a shop
with tools and metal and soldering, but then he,

hauling out his brain and skill cred, saying I can do this,
then, her *nah*, his *yup*; now she's all—you'll need

goggles, a helmet, mask for the fumes, earplugs for your hearing,
        and for your hands—good mitts, want my oven mitts?

Of course the protective vest—the kind that jockeys
wear on a Thoroughbred running forty miles an hour—and which

I can easily buy down at the racetrack—hold on, I'm driving
        there now, got my book on tape—about the endless creation

of St. Peter's, centuries of design, creation, then tear down;
travertine and marble, build again, gold, and tile;

       poison a pope here and there, windows, glass, thousands
of lives commencing, ending, copper plate, amazing doors,

many ducats paid out, the splendor of arch and fresco
and glorious bells in the evening tolling the hours.

After Confluence

The long, slim beans of the catalpa
shrivel in the heat, and even the grass looks hurt

beside American River's south fork,
which toys with the light and is quick and tumbling,
while from the valley, the north's dark fork

lumbers in full shadow and drinks in the light
with slow pleasure. People picnic,
drink beer, throw a Frisbee to the dog.

At the river's confluence, there's the merger
of two streams crashing, surging
in a whitewater glory,
which mysteriously, continuously,
rights itself, settles, and runs south.

Downriver you wouldn't know
that confluence held so much drama—
here where the slow river is sun-splashed,
boulder-strewn, sporting an alder tree
up to its ankles in water.

Under the distant sound of the train to Auburn,
a woman singes the air with her line,
reels and casts again, mumbling to the unseen,
Please try this one.

Damage

Damage, today I'm obsessed with damage.
The cored-out heart of the rose, not the bud
or the bloom, but root to flower—

whatever's maimed, blemished, blistered, harmed,
this skin the talon, the thorn has hooked—
morning's minion, ha—

and those shreddy clouds the sky assembles
only to have something fun
to tear into pieces. I remember Vuillard's painting, awash

with parlor knickknacks, his floral decor so chintzed
you can't tell carpet from chair from curtain, can barely see
the old woman dying quietly in her rocker.

Down the street, in the corner shop the hollowed slabs
of ribcage swing. From the café radio
Janis Joplin's ropy voice,
almost present, then static, then gone.

Something gleams from the hubcap, saying,
It's evening, you lived so *long,*
what have you done? Answer it back, oh hubcap,

some things can't be lived through—
the bolus we grow around—but there is
some endurable affliction,

the abscessed hoof sliced back until it bleeds;
we pack in the mud and wait and hope
enough foot grows back to nail on a shoe.

The long days are marked by waiting by the phone,
by the door, by the mailbox, and the sense
that the days themselves are passing.

Sunday Rain

There's a woman at my feet, with a mouthful
of pins, saying, *Nip the hem, dear,*
your ankles are your best feature,
show them off. Piranha woman.

Broken strings and wind through the reeds,
Sunday rain. *Slap palms together,*
mad as churchgoers, cake and coffee,
revelation to knock the sense into you.

Thoughts are a capsule
under the tongue, some days bitten open,
what's inside comes pouring forth. Come springtime,
flat the fifth and keep on playing.

Lightning's the Lord, she also explains,
come down to strut his stuff,
show them off, your best feature,
this kindly piranha woman.

The man in my morning café, saying, *Watch out,*
I'm having a little bitty rat terrier day,
watch your ankles, lady,
and announces he wants his coffee *dark, dark.*
So make it bitter, and keep the strings a-flying.

Listening to Seamus Heaney Read His Translation of Beowulf While at the Gym on the Elliptical Machine Quite Early on a Monday Morning

The badass dragon's done for, collapsed, out of form,
out of life, a grand deflation. The tatted homey next over,
huge headphones, loud on his cell; I evil-eye him; he desists.

Our hero is languishing, our old man
who's taken on the ravisher of life, hoarder of treasure.

(Note to self: Breathe, buy milk, pay bills, and heart rate's
way too high. Note to self: Chick on next machine
hurling sweat, coughs a frenzy; best avoid her.)

I'm the dragon, hoarding bright moments,
sharp words, glints of treasure, all for memory.

Beowulf at life's end, breath's end, beside his fiercest foe,
summoning the last words of solace, designing funeral rites,
his heritage, what's carried forward.

The Wednesday couple toddle in, fatter than — now words
fail me anyhow, they give the machines a workout.

All that gold—what's a dragon
want with gold, to bury it deep in earth, to take so many lives?

Old guy removes his shoes, weighs his scrawny body
as usual, sighs and works the daylights from the bike.

Still a dragon, here I go, stealing texture, faceting the edges,
turning it around in the light, hoarding all for later.

And Seamus Heaney's voice, calling me back to sound.
As day begins again I enter the chapel of his voice.

In This Afterlife

They walk, but it's not quite walking—
I'd say they approach, with eagerness, not exactly

as you remember them, but somehow
better—at ease—having arrived at the essential
comfort they longed for, so unattainable
        in life, and now stripped of all

that onrushing, kaleidoscopic existence, they've
acquired a simple presence, and as you step
        closer, it's evident they have each become
what you hoped for, as you have surely

turned into someone they envisioned,
your silliness and evasions, your rigidity included,
        but as you observe in their faces
an endless calm, where once there was boredom

        or rage, adoration or bemusement,
none of this matters, which is in itself a small sorrow,
that their old hunger for you
        to say something funny, sit for another hour,

and feed their slavering dogs, that's all gone now, and there
        isn't a thing you can offer them, and nothing
you can take back with you.

SWEPT UP ALL THE WORDS

Another Return

Yes, it was the hottest August anyone living
could remember when you came back for five days;
in the late afternoon, when the heat wore down,
the air freshened itself, the shadows uncurled, and you
came back as *a white butterfly*, assailed by three bees,
examined by a hummingbird. Your whiteness sharp
against the dark leaves, you floated and slipped —
the flight of any butterfly *so trite*, nailed into words —

even so, *listen up*, we think of you deep into winter,
when we need you the most, hefting your body
through the air with those complex wings, lightly,
it seemed, and we watched you drift from rose to basil
to heather, knowing we'd lose *this you*, and no matter
how often we close our eyes to see — you'd be gone.

Mnemonics of the Top Left Drawer

Always a new penny as a reminder for the one doled out
when I was small, with the words that if I kept on rubbing,
it would turn into *pure, swear-to-God-I'm-not-lying,*
actual gold. I still wish he'd rot in hell,
whoever he was. I remember his voice.

One chestnut swiped from the tree
outside Cézanne's studio, pocketed on my way
to stroll the studio with its props: the cloak,
walking stick, wrinkled apples, the day's
daily still life. I fiddle with my pilfered thing
and conjure the painter's most gorgeous, poisonous green.

And this, my Aladdin's lamplet, a half-full
blue glass bottle of Evening in Paris. Unscrew the lid,
and the scent ascends, the same cheap elegance
you can count on not to fade or transmute. It's a train
you can ride for miles.

A two-dollar losing show ticket from fifty years back.
A dark brown gelding. He didn't run well, came back
with that look for his groom, the dejected look a horse
can have of *Oh, boss, I did the best I could.* I wish
I'd kept track of him, knew what became of him.

The World as You Left It

The strands of hair in the brush and
the indentation in the pillow, your dog
snoring on the bed, the unkind note
on the dresser top, the red silk rose
the body guys left for us, the curtains
full of dust, swinging, as a bird lands
on the stone wall, the summer heat
bears down, and eight geese take off
from the pond, and as his backhoe idles,
the guy smokes, while in the distance
there's the endless hum of cars,
and a small plane sets loose a glider
in the afternoon, into the quiet
of all that space opening out.

All the space opening out
in the afternoon quiet, as overhead,
a small plane sets loose a glider,
and in the distance the endless hum
of cars, and nearer, the guy lighting
his smoke, his backhoe idle, as geese
rise from the pond, the summer heat
bearing down, a bird on the wall,
the curtains full of sunlight and dust,

in the room where the body guys left
a silk rose. An unkind note
on the dresser top, your dog snoring
on the bed, the indentation in the pillow,
and four strands of hair in the brush.

Postcard from Venice

To any of the others who are listening,
if, indeed, you bother listening, no offense.
I want to tell that other you about our trip,
which was mainly Baby Jesus in Ma's arms,
then Baby Jesus grown up, about his business,
washing some feet, hauling his cross uphill,

blood drops on his brow. I don't want to offend,
but in umpteen venues young Jesus on a cross,
breathing out his ghost, back in Ma's arms again,
though you, who never swooned over babies,
much less maternity, you'd have loved the dark,
the incense, the burst of sunlight on the canals.

But I can't send a postcard, can't call to tell you
about our hours, how they passed, how they're gone.

The Dishwasher's Late-Night Lament

The nightly congregation of crockery
slithering into the confessional bath—
Oh, hands, the plates sigh,
we've been smeared (Oh, oysters,

said the walrus, or the carpenter). Oh, mind—
where shall we go tonight, the table clean,
the talk complete. And you,

your meals, can you name them? A birthday,
greedy children, bright-candled roses,
all blue in buttercream, the faces lit,
quick wish, the blow-out.

Father, drying a platter, staring into it,
blowing, staring into his own reflected face—
a water mirror rippling shut—sealing him

into place. *A kid,* he says, *I'd go downstairs,*
and help dry the dishes—it was the main time
there was someone who'd talk to me.

The Dolls

The girl two farms over
had every imaginable kind. She had a roomful,
her shelves stuffed full of dolls. My desire to own
any one of them left me gasping for air.

It was clear that my perfect doll
would yield up its secret, the intimate knowledge
of the place where words come from,
and where they go to when there's no one
around to speak to them.

I would have settled
for the dumb-eyed raggedy doll, or the one
with the fat white porcelain hands, or the one
with the glassy blue eyes that rolled back in her head,
as if she might faint this instant.

I'd have killed to possess
that girl's lowliest doll. Okay, I was strange,
but admit it, you, too, were a weird little kid. Didn't you
ever have a need so sharp that if you tasted the edge of it,
your tongue might bleed?

No, the girl said,
you can't have any, they're mine, mine. But oh,
didn't—don't you—stumble out of her house,
squinting into the blazing daylight—hungry
for whatever was still out there, still hungry?

Dream

Of shaking a skeleton, demanding that it answer,
Of taking one breath then another,

That a voice commanded, *Be a fingerprint tracer,*

A theoretician of nothing,
That I swept up all the words my mother spoke,

We drove to Florida, got lost, then a man saying,
Venezuela, welcome to Venezuela,
That we searched the yard by flashlight for the objective correlative,

Of leaving home with a suitcase, on foot, by roller skate,
Horse, train, swimming through air ten feet above ground,
Of standing quietly in a line that wrapped three times
Around the Earth at the equator,

Of God saying don't worry so much about nightingales,
About an intruder who stole my vinegar, mustard, and hot sauce,
About a voice saying, *Fold the shirts your father owned,*
Fold those shirts again.

Inhabitation

It's when I'm climbing upstairs, late winter,
hauling myself up in that familiar shuffle,
grabbing the handrails, that I know I *become
the two of you*, in my own bent body,
lumbering upward, and wish you could see
this late, gorgeous sunlight. How I miss your voices,
your only bodily selves. I've no home movie,
no tape — the frail record stored in my brain.

I summon pieces and play them: of *this you*
grumbling about *the goddamn cold* while you
stomp the snow and stoop to set going, for us,
that blazing fire, while *the other you* limps down
to find a snack, your dozen gold bangles jangling,
as if some gaudy harem queen had just dropped in.

North

When my mother died, she chose to leave us
simply, without much fanfare, as they once said

of people who lived in the far north, who held
time within their bodies until they relinquished it.

She mentioned the cat by his name, turned her face
west, closed her eyes one evening in the August heat.

This I know. I also know that she set forth alone,
at daybreak, stepping out into fresh snow, clothed,

but past hunger, not wholly abandoned, but yes,
chosen, and choosing to go north, into more cold,

into a stark place and pure, without scent or sound.
North, I say, because for years I dreamt of traveling

far enough north to find silence and peace, and again,
she beat me to it, turned her face and closed her eyes.

I lose her tracks in the snow; I can't get there in time,
where death happens again, to her and to me.

Autumn All Over

For you to come back, it takes any small plane,
the faintest *puttputt* of it flying loopily over,
that plaintive noise in September, a few clouds
and sunlight, the plane skimming the field where goats
are browsing, horses nose the grass, but no more
the pear tree manic with bees—it gets to be a list
of the long-gones, doesn't it—you in your prime;

as I step into your years—that goldy haze of a guy
draped over an aqua Buick, your favorite dame
upstairs, your guys-in-the-know in town, two of us
in seersucker, shoveling the dirt, staring stupidly
up at you, only dimly aware of our own puny primes—
we'd have them one sweet day—moments we'd miss,
the hum of what's leaving—so long for now, small plane.

Electrical Tidings

That summer my main accomplishment
        was not breathing. I'd catch myself
working, cooking, not breathing; who knows where

the breath went — neither held, nor dispersed — it wasn't
within me. I lived in an airless world,
        scolding myself to suck in some gulps

of air, during that summer a few loved people
hadn't been dead so long that I didn't think about them
        every day, but gone long enough to talk to them
about the stupid things people did, or about

what I wrote, or regretted, and they, by then, telling me
what they missed most from the world. This was also
        the summer that the next-door ladies

put collars on Harold and Ida to lightly shock
their hearing when they barked — and these dogs barked
at nothing, all day, always at nothing —

and here's the thing: when Harold and Ida barked,
the electrical ringing went off in my head — really —
the sound happened in my skull, a high-wired noise,

intense, subtle, and piercing; I couldn't
escape, and though I could leave home, the noise
would be there, tapping its toes, waiting
to get going again, in my brain, in my breath,
as if it too owned my life that summer.

CAN'T YOU HEAR THAT FLOWER

Earning My Keep

Sold Almond Joys in eighth-grade snack shop,
nannied three brats, their mommy too,
one long Connecticut summer. Spent time
checking in your general psychotics, schizoids,
your ruined and wracked at a local county bin.

And spent the greatest summer of a life
and pieces of many years hosing the legs
of Thoroughbreds, wrapping their legs,
scrubbing buckets, flinging hay, brushing
the lustrous shoulders and gleaming flanks . . .

And during my interminable loser phase,
sold girdles — not well — at 22nd and Mission,
drove a school bus through Chinatown, eyes shut
downshifting four, three, two — carried mail,
possibly yours, cursing your stupid catalogs,

and bussed dishes, took your orders, *Sir,*
what would you prefer, or *Ma'am, may I suggest* . . .
Sold books, *Shall I put it on hold for you?*
listened for decades into the undertones
of the distressed. In short, I earned my keep.

Goldfish

I won them shooting wooden rabbits at the fair.
Willingly, each rabbit gave itself to the shot cork.
Winning felt brilliant and painful as ice
held against teeth.

Three goldfish in a glass bowl, a horizon
between their water, my air, a boundary
that could be jiggled.

They ate my brew: wings of a fly, petal of aster,
chewed-up flake of oat. Endured incantations:
don't die today, don't die tonight.

The first television carved a niche with images
of history floating through the house, the Rosenbergs' faces,
after the screen went blank. It was something

about stolen words and the touching of live wires
that made orphans of the Rosenberg kids.
The fish outgrew their bowls, and on a gnat-filled
August day, three cold fires were set free in the pond.

Their descendants were pale, slack-jawed
bottom-feeders.

Other people bought the farm and slicked it up.
If they ever dredge the pond, a huge, satin-flanked
ghost fish will rise to greet them.

Fox Piss

I bought it to safeguard my one-twelfth of an acre
from a grabby squirrel, a twitchy-eyed scavenger
who raided and pillaged my bird feeders. I'd failed
with sprinkling cayenne, flunked with pricy baffles,
with greasing the poles, and beaten again, had sprung
for the AK-47 of squirt guns, blasting to smithereens
the blood-red blooms of my Mr. Lincoln, his velvety,
perfume-drenched petals falling pathetically around me.
You think I'm kidding? No squirrel is cute, and nature
be damned. I want shrieking sparrows and furious finches
battling mid-air for a sunflower seed, my dumb-eyed doves
lolling in the dust. Though whatever I want is unattainable,
I fell for yet another promise: I'd mimic the predator. *They*
promised I'd attain stewardship of my tiny domain!
Once more I'd be indomitable mistress of my kingdom!
They didn't warn me about spillage — about the genie out
of the bottle — its stench, the reek of something so primal,
so essentially archaic, condensed to a droplet, suffusing
every pore. My family shunned me, and my pals have left.
My turf is secure, but believe me, friend, I'm stained for life.

Her Garden, 1968

It seemed unkind that day,
her sudden anger
about one flower — something
yellow, something
casually wanted,
while we walked together,
chatting about the world,
and when that flower
didn't instantly yield
was quickly twisted
until stem and blossom
severed, were wrenched
free. She was old and spoke
in that blunt Kentucky voice,
You'll never do that
again. You'll sharpen
shears, make a clean cut;
can't you hear that flower
screaming at you? No, I said,
then, I can't. *Flowers are*
forever, she said, *you are not.*

His Back Forty

How desperately he begged for *weed*
that one Christmas I spent on the farm
in Kentucky, long-gone now, him as well,
he needed those seeds for Grandmother

to germinate, to transplant to back acres
nourishing soybeans — until *"the goveʹment"*
paid more to plow crops underground
than the world paid for people

to sell good beans — wanted *weed* for ducks
that adored the stuff, for the fine, fat ducks
of autumn; he hoped they'd land, and gorge,
and be dreamily ready for his shotgun.

As for seeds — no source! I, what's worse,
planned on being *someone*, getting *somewhere*,
was barely dazzled by the two of *them*,
so old, such schemers, still wanting everything.

I'd Have Liked Some Dinner

That was the night when my father—I hadn't seen him
in years—was to meet me in Manhattan, certain place,
certain hour, you've already guessed it, the hours,
they passed, before the phone—that voice—
drunk and mumbling—he'd lost the last two numbers

of my number and tried every combination, voilà!
And olé! He reached me! Could I get there and did I
have any money? Oh well, yes, I sausaged myself
into the dark-blue wool—quite proper—and walked
forever to the 21 Club where Dad was being tossed
out—raging, whining—I hadn't, I've told you already—

seen him in years. The polite, oily men in tuxedos
stuffed him into a taxi; we drove around, him hungry
to show me, to have me know his old spots uptown—
where most back then weren't dumb enough to tour
at midnight. He tapped the driver to idle, nudging me,

Here I danced Saturday nights, smoked the wicked weed
here, a dame, up there, he said, as I sat there, cringing.

Driving West after Sunset

Before dusk, defined as the *darker part of twilight*,
but before twilight, which is deemed
the *deepening obscurity,*

the setting sun was a golden coin, dropping into
the blanched horizon slot. I drive into
that white space, called the *afterglow.* Day's end
has come to the dry-baked Valley ground.

Sami, the radio psychic, owns the air tonight,
nailing the future with her breath: *He's the one,*
she tells her caller, *expect your diamond by fall . . .*

She doesn't tell the next one her child will overdose,
her man will leave, her mother wander the house,
mumbling to God, waiting for years for a phone to ring.

The West, turning colorless, hauls me toward it,
miles from where I had dinner with my friend,
where all types of barbed wire, sharp bits, and spurs,
quirts, and skinning knives could be seen on display

as we talked about how, in Harlow's monkey tests,
his monkey babies — offered a choice — preferred
clinging to cloth mothers rather than to wire ones.

And they preferred wire mothers
to none at all. All through dinner our waitress
was reluctant to bring things: *Some bread? And a spoon?
Ummm, water?* she struggled, poor thing.

The rituals of being alive seemed for those hours
enormous and also inconsequential. And now twilight,
which is elsewhere defined, deepens to an inky blue.

Crossing the Whole Country

There's turbulence, the plane suffering mood swings,
the good ones floaty, but you can't count on them.

Always trust your pilot, says the Air Force flier beside me,
commuting to war, to this war,
to this war he cheerfully enters, he who is a squirrel-eyed boy
with a skin-soft voice.

Now the bad mood is lasting forever,
the plane slamming the sky as if it, too, were a body.

Fear scrambles my prayer: *Daily bread, cup running full,
the hallowed and bring me, Lord, out of this valley, please.*
Hesiod says, *Wash your hands before libation.*

The Air Force kid says *in the desert,* his *mother plane's*
gravid belly is stuffed with helicopters and missiles,
and assures me that, *real high up,*
you're knocking on the doorway to heaven,

but that's where I imagine frozen Mallory crouched
on the world's roof, snow goggles still in the inside pocket
of his good tweed suit,

then I think of Shackleton's men,
after *The Endurance* foundered and keeled,
shooting the puppies, then the dogs, then eating them,

even though they had names: Toby, Nelly, Roger.

The plane is being rung out again
like the sky's dishrag.

To distract me, our Air Force guy peels back his shirt,
tilts his neck, exposing a sprung clavicle, a
cantilevered breastbone — from a knife, a bullet?
Perhaps he wants me to remember

his nearly submissive gesture, not just the yellow umbrellas
he told me they fix to each bomb,
briefly delaying the downward path.

Feather on the breath. Nothing else I can offer him.

COMBING THE PASTURE FOR A HORSE

Memory Palace

Sometimes you start with the room, that place
of four walls, the door, tall windows looking out,
one to the west, one south, enough light for joy.
Sometimes you have to start with the room itself
and not worry how the hours passed, how the room
belongs to the house, which you know quite well —
the staircase, hallway, the radiator's rattle, and smell
of garlic frying, voices from the den and laughter
from the yard — but you start with the room, how it
holds so much of you — your breathing, your sleep,
your reveries and endless waves of dread — you glance
out the window for beauty: a cloud, there's nothing
like a cloud with its belly lit gold and rose at sunset;
you're grateful for this room you come back to again.

First Knowing

Maybe in God's world, it was dark, then light,
but know that in my world, light was the sole
progenitor — always in motion, arriving or slipping
away, fathoming this meadow, that pond,

carving the hill's bright crest. You couldn't tell
them apart, light from place, they inhabited the mind
so deeply, light that sculpted September evenings,
those two people mowing here, raking there,

the glow that warmed their faces as they puttered
around their world. And how this world imprinted
itself on us — canny, uncanny — space calling on light
to enliven its whole body, and sunlight after sundown.

Evening, No Moon

The same red fox at sunset
jogs across the road, past the pond where the ducks
      utter small notes of contained hysteria.

Indoors, a phone rings five times,
a bored voice growls — *Yeah, well, okay then.*
Floorboards creak, the fridge sighs open,
      sighs shut, as ice cubes rattle around

a glass, last bird calls from the dogwood.
When I was young, I stood here smoking and fiercely
      wanting — *what?* — something

out of reach. That was then. It's time now for our bats —
      useful, sinister — to flee their stinky lairs,
our little Penelopes, who fling themselves

into the night, which they rip to shreds,
though by dawn they've stitched up — for the moment.

Memory Palace II

The only picture left of the two of us
is gone. I barely owned it a few weeks, that's all.
I must have stuck it in a book somewhere.
And yes, I ransacked those books for that image
burned into my brain, which we know will fade
in time, but still, I can't find the picture I had
from years ago, when you looked so happy
as we went walking. I was proud, and the day

was beautiful. I make this up from memory—
not remembering the day we went walking—
I only remember the picture. I had it and lost it,
carrying now the image, the two of us, strolling
in dresses, at the track. I was small. The day
must have been sunny. I've lost my only picture.

Wait for Me

Thin light on the path ahead,
        wavering, can't see it,
now here again, your footsteps,
the starlight faint, fireflies' light
muffled in the humid night air.
Can't make out that sound—
bird, maybe animal, no matter,
a living being, a comfort.
You've gone on ahead,
following you is often boring,
        exhausting, occasionally
thrilling—there's a moment's
respite to hear the creek's
thin trickle, to smell the watercress
        crushed underfoot—so bright,
so bitter. Wait for me, I'll catch up
with you, any day now.

Greetings to You from Today

And when that neighbor had two more babies,
she brought them home with such a puzzled look
on her face, and down the street another neighbor
dropped dead, and out back two others yell at night,
but only at 3 A.M., and the helicopters, they *shlup-shlup*
the air at noon because of the redwood tree-sitters
who've been pelting the arborists with poop.

How you would have laughed, hungry to hear of this life
with its goings-on. You with your *acres* of pasture,
What did you know, we once thought, about the world
in its handbasket of storms and wars, this unfolding
mysterious world. We're growing old now, peering out;
we're glittering bits of sand in the palm of someone
else's hand. Come back and tell us what we need to know.

Boxwood Hedges

Gorgeous — the boxwood hedges, seven feet tall —
then when you slashed them down, we were grateful;
you left us a steeplechase run for summer evenings,
and we kids trained hard to win, urging one another —
fast and eager alike — to run the course, to one hedge,
bend sharp, a hedge, take back, then make a move,
and on to win, stopping to sip from the spigot's water,
driven — what rough mix of human and horse, we kids —

in the heat until dusk, spent and pausing to drink again
from the cool springhouse flow; you called us home
at the first star, the last dog barking and Ike still prez;
all the while, poison leached into our water, arsenic
from our neighbor's orchard dripped into our ground,
arsenic for his apples. We packed up, we made it out.

Beyond Our Borders

East of the meadow lived a sad white dog
whom we called Bagsy Eyes (owned by the family
on the tracks). He haunted our farm for daily chow.
And to our west lived the farmer we called Weasel,
who sneakily sent his cattle across our fence line
for clover; at our northern border, a family
of *misfortunates*, the forlorn girl-child trudging
uphill from the school bus. We fretted about them

long before, one by one, they each succumbed
to our regional cancers, but beyond our boundary
to the north, it was all Baker's Woods; we muttered,
"Who the hell was Baker?"